CW01652418

# CHARLI CHIMPANZEE

By Tony Mitton

Illustrated by Martin Chatterton

CAMBRIDGE
UNIVERSITY PRESS

Charlie Chimpanzee wanted some honey to eat.
He wanted some honey from the bees.
So he looked to see if the bees were all asleep.

Charlie Chimpanzee was greedy.
He wanted lots and lots of honey.
"I hope it's nice and sweet," he said.

He looked at the bees' home on the branch of the tree. But he didn't see that the bees were there.

The Queen bee was very angry. She looked really mean. She wanted to teach Charlie not to steal.

Charlie went up to the bees' home and put his hand through the hole. Then he poked a pole into the hole, and then he poked his nose into the hole!

But an angry bee stung Charlie on the nose.
"Ow!" squeaked Charlie.

He began to moan and groan.
"Now I'll have to put cream on my nose!" he cried.

Charlie still wanted a tasty treat. So he started to dream about lots of things he could eat.

“Let’s see.
There’s toffee.
There’s coffee.
There’s hot, roast meat.
There’s peaches and cream,
and loaves that steam . . .
and toast to eat.”

What Charlie liked most was toast. Toast was a real treat. But he didn't like eating toast without honey!

Just then, he heard the bees buzzing.
The branch had broken, and their
home was in the stream!

Charlie ran as fast as he could,
and he reached the stream just in time.

The bees came back and they were very pleased with Charlie. The Queen Bee came to meet him and she said,

“Look at this, Chimpanzee.
Look what the bees have got for you to see.
It’s what you like most,
to put on your toast.
It’s yellow and sweet.
A real treat!”

"Oo-whee!" cried Charlie.
"Is this for me? Sweet, yellow honey?
Whoopee!"